M000012900

I have to live.

BOOKS BY AISHA SASHA JOHN

The Shining Material (2011)
THOU (2014)
I have to live. (2017)

I have to live.

poems

aisha sasha john

McClelland & Stewart

Copyright © 2017 by Aisha Sasha John

All rights reserved. The use of any part of this publication reproduced, transmitted in any form or by any means, electronic, mechanical, photocopying, recording, or otherwise, or stored in a retrieval system, without the prior written consent of the publisher — or, in case of photocopying or other reprographic copying, a licence from the Canadian Copyright Licensing Agency — is an infringement of the copyright law.

LIBRARY AND ARCHIVES CANADA CATALOGUING IN PUBLICATION

John, Aisha Sasha, author
I have to live / Aisha Sasha John.

Poems.
Issued in print and electronic formats.
ISBN 978-0-7710-5070-1 (paperback). – ISBN 978-0-7710-5071-8 (epub)

I. Title.

PS8619.O444I12 2017   C811'.6   C2016-904537-4
                                              C2016-904538-2

Published simultaneously in the United States of America by
McClelland & Stewart, a division of Penguin Random House Canada Limited,
a Penguin Random House Company

Library of Congress Control Number is available upon request

ISBN: 978-0-7710-5070-1
ebook ISBN: 978-0-7710-5071-8

Cover design by Rachel Cooper
Cover image: © Tuja66 / Dreamstime.com

Typeset in Requiem by M&S, Toronto
Printed and bound in the USA

McClelland & Stewart,
a division of Penguin Random House Canada Limited,
a Penguin Random House Company
www.penguinrandomhouse.ca

1   2   3   4   5   21   20   19   18   17

THIS BOOK IS DEDICATED TO THOSE WHOM IT IS FOR.

AND TO MY DAD.

Contents

THREE

RAT VS. LAMB

FIVE

What would I write if I were going to live?

One

Something softens me

Softens my desire
Something helps me breathe
Something spills out my pores as light
Something
Is like hope blanketing me
Something bleeds as me:
Tea on the cuff
Of a blouse in the day
Lazing at the sink.
I scratch my head to flakes.
I return to
My reading.

The first knowledge is of our ignorance.
Hi.

What's seeable and not
I join
For those to whom I'm betrothed.

I am the bride of your listening.

And a withering pear I can't eat.

It's messy.
I have to eat.
Because I love.
I put my life on my body.
It's hungry.
I do it
Because it's hungry.
I'm lazy
And I barely even read.

Why should I know what I'm talking about
When I can merely feel it?

You have to worship the fact of life and not its
Corny by-products.

Art is for romantics.
Art is for stupid people.

It's believable.
When you sin it is believable.
You have the evil fingers.
You have creation light, too.
You've been so sorry.
Why have you been sorry?
Think about what life has done to you.
When you think the good are to be rewarded
You reveal your essential stupidity.
I am asking you to take that cover
Down.
I hate a white sky, bare trees, Ontario-ness, winter.

I keep saying I submit and do not.
I have to attend to my pussy.
I have to attend to my heart.

It's true I hardly know what's going on
And can't let that full fact go.
I've let my thoughts virgo as
Detective work
Though I have to have problems I suppose
To tenderize
My sweetness.
Or else I would have a
Very, very hard sweetness.

Considering

As a way of being.
I have done that.
A decided
Closeness
With the
Materials
Of a circumstance.
I like have been close to
What's arrived and
Arriving: I saw
Everything.
And I listened to
Some, many.

I listened to a great deal
And with a placid intelligence
Supported
The odours entering me.

I smelled; thus
I knew.
I could smell
In this Friday blue hour –
An approach to
Night as it
Isn't night:

I can't see the sky
From where I'm sitting
But I see
The colour of the air
Around the cactus
And the colour of the air
Around the
Red soil
And I know what the sky is thinking:
I see it turn itself
To closing, so I –
Good night –
Can leave this room
Where the vibration of a resting cellphone
Is a fart
In the, now,
Night –

I have to live. There's stuff inside of things.

There's a fridge in the staff kitchen.
And there's stuff inside that fridge
That isn't for me to eat but I want
To eat it.

A sound.
Is there
Someone behind me?
No ok I want to eat what I left at home then.
I am glad that I left it
So that
I can eat it –

The centre of a blackberry
It's like eating butterfly body, basically.

What is bread?

Is bread women?
Is bread youth?
Is bread sorrow?
Is bread
A marshmallow?

What is bread?

In the dream

I didn't want to give him the $20 on my dresser.

Days before there weren't
And then were snakes
Of blue, red, and lemon
Ejecting from a hedge
Maze, a garden.

I want on a walk.
I want
Every morning
The damp, loose soft
Of the sky.

I sleep in a room.

I store clothing there.
Outside my room is a hallway
That leads to a door
Beyond which
Is a street
In a city
In a world
In which I live too.
I live in this world.
I live
Today.

I'm of a time.
It will know its name when
It is over.

When I am dead this time
Will be an object
And I
Will be an object
Too.

That's okay.
Right now I am alive
And
I like it.

My boobies are soft.

There's a vast
Coldness behind my waist.

The sky.

In my nipple is an eye.

I would do it.
I would do it like you.
I could have it.
I could have it like you.

I am in love.

But I only cry about it when I'm hungry.
When I die I'll just be me again
And soft.
I look outside.
A city street.
I look at it. I am it.
I look outside.
I have to.
Because I

Like everything.

Dec 31, 2014

I have left prime sweetness
Between the tight teeth
Of some hurried days.

Let me now keep it.
Jeez, it's the année's
Final creeping night.

My name is A'isha
But has it
Kept its promise.

I lie on the bed.
I lie very still.
I cry.

Aquamarine and topaz

Cast as the eyes of
Sick and slow-moving cats.

I was high and I was lost.

I was slow and found
I was low and found.

Everywhere there are men, there are men

Loving other adults.
And everywhere
There are women
Same.

When we were alone in the night
The light
Of your small shop called me.

I bought bottled water
And a loofah.

And then dans la même square the next day
He said
No, I said
No, wait –
He said,
D'Afrique?
Des Caraïbes, I say, Mais
Oui. I point to the rhombus
That's the back of my hand:
La même chose.
Who said that?
I don't even know
If you said it or if
I said it.

You said it.
And then I said
Hamdulillah
And you said
Hamdulillah
Too.
I went
South.

I forget.
I remember: ok
The thing
Wasn't that it was tight
And that I was breaking out of a case
And transiting forms
And that there was a cover that
Cracked
And the line
Was the tear of that
The rip in that was the line –
No.

The caterpillar actually dies
Becoming the whatever.

A line.
It is a fiction.
An idea
Of direction.
An index.

The line.
An idea I breathed
Automaton-ically
Across campus
And shook –
Wearing heeled boots to class
Who did I meet but
A rectangle of
International development gals.

The motherfucking line.

The blood
Runs from where it begins
Into the lake that's
My left foot.

It feels like
Wind inside me.

When I leave here I don't know where I am.

I read the map wrong and got lost.
So I was home.
When I was physically lost that was home so I am crying.
I'm not crying.
The reason I'm not crying is I don't care.

I warmed some hash in butter and wiped a yellow square of cake into it deeply.
And I put it in the mini fridge and the next morning, the next
Afternoon –
I ate it.

"Slowness is a formidable power;
It has the passion of immobility
With which it will someday fuse."

Number one – and
Two:
That to study philosophy
Is to learn how to
Die.

Two

I like it when we give the world to itself

Folding it to it
Like a soft-shelled taco. Hi, God.

I said in the photo's caption.
It's Aisha.

I volunteer.

I do.
I did it.
I did.
I had to.
I have to.
I have to live.

Ruth taught me M.G.'s dance in which one imagines herself held by a giant blue woman named Eureka

The performance of which
Begets the knowledge that I'd been dancing as if
Alone
An axial dance
Rotating on a centre inside myself (like a stick or a stalk) but with
Eureka behind me
The axis was everywhere
Which made me think of my mom

So I b-lazed
And then shaking upward from the floor to my crown felt
Generations of pain.
And then an image of my mother laughing hard and bright
Quizzed me
And from my feet again
To, this time, my halo
Generations-of-joy waves
Pulsed
And a door swung open in the centre of my chest
Revealing a giant passage
For of
Love
I can
Could now
Take it.
That was June.

I can't believe I agreed to go to work today.

That was so dumb of me.
I hate money.
And I hate sitting down.

I fold in half

Documents destined for the shredder.

I leave flat the ones to be scanned into patient charts.

I consider how long stickers have rested on the glass
Protecting me from potential
Disease and violence
Of the people.

The first time I came here I was late, I was scolded
I was bleeding.
I barely even cared
Fuck, look:
When I start to bleed
I have to eat.

One headline said 5 minutes early is on time;

On time is late; late

Is unacceptable.

The other headline said optimists are usually late.

The last said cultural differences

Around time something-something.

I took a screenshot.

I wonder what the point is though when I can

Merely live.

I am an angel but I respire.

I drink a cold red juice.
It's Sunday in the truth study centre remember when I was sleeping, freezing
And so put my cashmere coat on upside down?
And reached down and from the floor of your room
There black and soft inside my grip was a jacket made of rabbit and I made my
Face and shoulders smooth in it?

"The Bay Area"

The hallway.
It was a good hallway – light. It had air.
I said to her our destiny
Is beyond this hallway – and
What did we see outside?
A man.
I climbed to his stoop and I sat beside him.
I rubbed his back. He was old
And small.   '
He was telling me something important
That I don't remember
But I remember that then he said something that made me stop
Rubbing his back.

She said my breath smelled like ice cream.

We went to Golden Gate Park's Botanical Garden and ate them.
And stretched on the lawn
Awaiting their arrival and then they came.
All the while we had excellent timing.
When she stretched her lower back on the grass I took
Photos in which her nose looks unlike it does actually.
I braided her whole entire head on the bench
And she let me
Saying
She felt as if she looked like
Felicia
From *Friday*.
They affected my hands such that I could arrive at the heat
Her hands emitted to a sensor in my own cold palm that was
Larger than touch.

She shook at me when I tried to
Help with the hoodie and I cried
Inside and late.

I cried in the night and morn
Because I was
Confused.

I met David Brazil. I bought *The Ordinary*.

Advanced Adulthood

I take a walk.
I order 3 tacos.
I order 2 tacos.
I take a walk.

What's the big fucking deal about

******* anyway.
It's empty there.
I didn't see anything there.
Where is it?

Today I could aspire but I want to nap

And look for the pot I lost in the desk I found on the street.
Some people are interested in exploring the ways
Something is negotiated
In light of something else.
God bless them.
I have to fucking live.

My north node placement
Suggests I shouldn't concern myself
With the thoughts or values
Of other people –
Which I understand to mean I mustn't antagonize "people" in my poems
Feeling triumphant in
Disputes I begin and leave the crust of but
Eat the cheese.

I had a vision now.
It wasn't a vision.
A man in a striped shirt stood in a line.
His hair looked like yours
So I thought of you.
Fuck I prolly should've messaged you back
After I asked for and you sent me that photo
Of your baby.

Your yes, yes.

Your no, nah.

Truth
Over evil.

I gotta go.

I gotta dream.
So that the Lord will
Find my finger.

Adornment is exaltation enacted.

I am an earring of the Lord.

It's Saturday. I meet you, get soft.

I have to trust people
Or else I'm too busy.

I feel nothing but foolish
And also okay
Because what will happen is I will
Continue to live.

And then one day I'll die.

I spread butter on the darkest rye

As if it's cheese.
A turd of butter
Attaches to the pen with which I write
This. I wonder if it's sanitary
To leave the ketchup outside all the time.
At night, even.
And also the hot sauce.

My duty is to tend

To the children I house
But I have hate in me.

I wake up.
It is a jealous dream.

The left side of my pussy
Hurts even.

He thinks I should be glad because they

Like the idea of Aisha. I am not the idea of Aisha.

I am Aisha.

You I know you

Love the idea of Aisha.

I am not the idea of Aisha.

I am not the idea of Aisha.

I am Aisha.

His thumbs were

So big also his fingers.
He was holding Gran's hand so as to take
What no one can give.
Relax yourself, she said.
She was dying. But he was sick.

Because I was being flown to Kelowna for a reading and he lives in Nelson

I thought I would visit him.
I didn't tell him this.
Perhaps I should have told it to him.
I thought it would be generous
Of me to
Keep it as a surprise
Instead of
Offering
It
As a promise.
Anyway, he fell off a cliff. And she stopped breathing.
They both stopped breathing
For the purposes of death.

To speak of which to you is
Blasphemy. Like
Who
Are you even?
Do you
Love me?

Regardless

If I am judged
If I am punished
If I am dismissed
If I am misunderstood
If I am celebrated
If I am envied
If I am competed with
If I am slandered against
If I am seen
If I am soft
If I am stupid
If I get it
If I surpass
If I intimidate
If I confound
If I confuse
If I'm confused
If I impress
If I delight
If I contradict
If I embarrass
If I'm transparent
If I'm arrogant
If I reproach
If I lamb
If I snake ssss
If I coconut
If I'm crazy
If I'm coo-coo
If I'm weary
If I resist
If I'm easy

If I'm wrong
If I'm wrong – who gives a fuck?

I have to live.

Three

In August I visited my Gran.

I.

I walk past the psychiatric hospital.
It's Sunday.
The beach was nice.
The sky is black.
I'm home.

At the nightclub they'd found five guns
And a lot of scissors.

When I read that to my mom she hears seizures.
Write a poem, she says.
Something
They can read at the funeral.

Today as I write this it is Thursday.
The funeral
Was last Saturday.
I did not send a poem.

Mama, I am a poem.

So yeah: the beach was nice; the sky is black.
I'm home.
There are headscarves on my aunties.
A man with hands like
Earth leads the service.

I look at his hands.

He ejects certain words as a way of singing.
Some get pushed
Out or are pulled.
They leap
Or are
Grabbed – I dunno.

On the television
A woman carves from a stack of rice krispie squares
Human breasts.

I feed cut watermelon to my grandmother.

I am low and found; I am high and found.
When I read that part to my mom over the phone she
Cries. It's sad
She says.

I put my ticket there on her Visa.

The next day my cousin sends me a message.
I read the message.
Then what I do is call my mother.
Now you don't have any more grandparents!

II.

The curtains in my grandmother's room are embroidered.
And peach.
And round and wild with wind.

A soft grey sky: Bye.
The crying I do at my cousin's shoulder
Is not even mildly shy.
We're yoked.
I think that's pretty.
I hold her
For a long time and she
Pats me. There are only
Two poems:

You write a letter.
Or you describe something.

I kiss
A soft face for the quote unquote
Last time.

She said to save some for myself.
And not to laugh with all my teeth.

Strong basic love

Names a doctrine
An orientation
A location
Within a relation
An arrangement –
Strong
Basic love
In silk
As yellow
On a cake-shaped
Black cap
I will custom-make
As a shield
I hold my own hand firmly

Look at us
I am holding you in my face

Look at me

Happy Cup

I scream a note.
I scratch my cheek.
And the Christ said
Eloi, Eloi,
Lama sabachthani.
I know every seed.
I know seeds.
I had a strawberry plant, clearly.
On the balcony.
They tasted good.
I have a family I keep.
So I'm really
Happy.

Round windows, wood bracelets, Xmas broaches, little fish.

A mammal with a tongue like a pencil.

I'm not sure.
But I am sure.
The lily is sure.
The rose bush.
Then there are leaves people bleed on.
I amn't sure.
But I am juice.

Spicy your life
The sign says:
Happy Cup Bar and
Restaurant.

You of age?
The proprietor asks me.
And then gestures
To the bathroom where stands my date.
And him?
As in the man pissing
With a dick I will never see.

The man was downstairs pissing
From what remains
A mystery.

Someone a woman says let's hug.
I reach for her hands.
Everybody has tetanus, she says, No.

Oh I feel great.
And jealous.
Ya I feel grealous.
I have ten minutes.
Today I want clarity.
I understand the next book cover
To be my tiny little ear so
If you want more instruction, note:
I already told you
To lie on the ground or
Sit on it.
It can't be
Saturday morning
All the time.

I defer to you.

It's great.
I'm tired of always knowing everything.
I know I'm wrong but I wish I were kidding.
Can my new used coat be my costume?

I invented pasta.
I invented cheese.

Blood

I've tried being lowly.
It doesn't fucking work.
I need
Love lest I
Be fucked up.

I look high
To receive my fate.
The world
It has not killed me.
I am after
Irreverence.
Today I fill a
Book with blood.

The problem is there's none.
I'm foolish enough.
And healthy as a mole.

I look up
To receive my fate.

A man's stride looses his hands to the day
Like a dollop of hollandaise.
He's alive. I am alive.
I have to
Live.

Angels rest in the cups of my clavicles.
Because there's no beef between stupid and hallowed.
There's no war
Between happiness and grief.

I keep thinking that I have a self
And in that
Do not love.
My burdens
Are a fiction.
What there's been
Is non-stop being.
It's Friday.
I gather to an end
Memories –
I have a narrative.
I commit to it. It's painful.
I collect because I have
Loved pain.
It's glorious.
And real.
I just
Know about it.
Apparently.

So if love
Is a technology
For sex
How betrayed my body has been
By my confusion.

I like it to be wild of heart and happy.
I like it to be happy.

Who am I
In this essay on the failures
Or inadequacies
Of sexual optimism?

It's radical
To take the essential good out of sex
The essay says.

I know that's very stupid.
I feel it is stupid
Deep inside my pussy.

Sex constitutes my body as woman.

What it means
To require that theatre is personhood.
The condition of which
Is gender.

To fuck
Or be fucked
Is
To appear.

I make clothing decisions
(they're unsuccessful)
On a Friday. It's May.
Something pulses around me.
Pulsing
Locates my pubis
As a site of recent activity.
I was a person.
I have an opening.
It's soft.

Look –
There are crickets in the lizard's tank.
They make the noise of being alive.

Some of the crickets are in a tower-shaped plastic container.
The kind you put cereal in if you do that.
There are carrot shavings
And a crumpled-up egg carton
In the plastic cage of the crickets –
So they might eat and perch
And live to die.

They feed
To be
Food.

I myself eat shaved carrots in a stir-fry.
I don't live in a cereal container.
But basically I do.
Anyway I have to live.

An essay challenges the good of pleasure.
I write the person I want to love.
Perhaps I am hasty
Or I am stupid, for
The Sagittarius
Hunts.
I look to her restraint for freedom.
Meanwhile I am love incarnate
All the time.
I came
To lay burdens down
But I don't have any –
I'd taken memories to the day as a tool for pity.

Pity. An ugly world and an ugly way.

Something with nails holds the couch cushion.
It is a lizard.
Because I get close
Its red eye's on me.

I have no burdens to lay down
Because I have no fricking story.

I lie down
So as to uncrease
My capable shoulders –
I have shirts. Crisp shirts.
Anyway,
I remember the despair
Duty put inside my night –
I remember a dreamscape
Of a freshly dead mouse at my bedside.
Yeah, how am I supposed to
Dispose
Of a burden?

In the future
A mouse does die.
It lies upon the dusk
Blue of my kitchen floor
Its face entirely semi-human I mean I just
Ran.

The superintendent.
I hid in the hall while he did the stuff.

Two days later I scrubbed from the floor
A teardrop-shaped stain.

It smelled like meat.

Rat vs. Lamb

A beach.

The northeast coast of a country.
What happened was a man.
A man came.
Onto the beach and then
Another
Came.
He wanted to.
The day
Might have made me sorry.
I left, saw
At the base of a palm tree
A rat.

I was born and I lived

Swishing fluoride around my mouth with the others.
From various classmates, I stole
Blue scissors, a hamburger sharpener, ten bucks.
My mom found the ten bucks.
She beat me.
I'm sorry
The teacher told me to say to Mandeep.
So I said, crying, I'm sorry, Mandeep.

I wore a mint-green Donna Karan suit
in the Lincoln LS commercial.

The makeup lady put concealer on my knuckles.
My husband
Was played by an NHL player whose mom was a white lady.
(He brought her to set!)
I got five grand, was nine
Teen, saw a Maybelline model
On the way back from the bathroom plus a flasher's
Wobbling dinky:
"Happy Canada Day."

I really like covering my head.

The landlord said he lost his phone.

The tenant she said call it.
He said I did, I did
And then the tenant's boyfriend was like
I called you and a girl picked up and
Said it was the wrong number.
(And I'm like okay so it was the wrong number why are you even
Telling the guy that)
And then her boyfriend was like ya, I called it four times
She said it was the wrong number.
And then, then I was like okay. Hmm what the fuck.
And the tenant was like maybe it was your wife?
And her boyfriend was like no it
Was a girl.
So there's a
Question there.

Also apparently the dog likes the cat
But the cat
Does not like the dog.

I want to walk the park with you

And look at the wondering people.

My neck.

My scalp.

I read somewhere that

It's okay.

One kind of pork or –

Another kind of pork.

May I recommend the ones we

Already have?

Oh ya

I'm not coming because I don't want to.

That's why I'm not coming.

Three hundred dollars for a half-leather belt.

With blue fish on it.

I thought you said it was a novella.

My neck.

My wick.

A man keeps three decades of nail clippings in a jar.

Chartreuse or mustard

Solid or see-thru:

The loose, wide stripes

On a girl.

Purse blacker than her shorts.

Hi.

Chicken/egg.

I need to take a dump.

Part of me doesn't believe it will work.

Who are people? Who are anybody?

It takes so long to know anything.

And it takes even longer

To know anything at all.

The pork chop is cold because I won't heat it.

It's breakfast.

It is breakfast.

I'm scared.

I take a medicine.

My sweet little
Coconut face falls.

The reds.
Pale yellow.
Screaming.

When I wash my feet at night
I'm cleansed of
Everything stupid.

I decided that I was a planet and I was a planet.

I had to.
I decided that I was a planet and –
I am.

I want to love.
I see old women
Who live.

They know something.

It's true I've suffered
The delusion
That I am unlamblike.
But oh my gosh that's crazy.

Though it doesn't matter where I sit
And that I'm fucking crazy.

God gave it to me.
I have to live.

It doesn't matter where I sit
And that I'm fucking crunchy.

I have to be fibrous
So as not to be consumed.
I have to
Fucking live.

I *can* live –
In the world –
With the people.

I can live in the world with the people if they understand that
All a poet is is some bitch
Who thinks she's better
And feels sort of bad about it
But not, not really that bad more like
Feels bad
For feeling bad
At all.

Also, I need a lot of money.
So I could have a lot of money.
That's why I need it.

I need a lot of money.
So I can have it.
Because I need to have money.

The crease

In the jeans
At the top
Of her thighs.

The pink and red
Oily flora
Of this
Bus-riding man's
Nose.

The hard snow cone of his belly.

Did you see us?

We were in June.

Westbound.

I looked at his bracelets.

The flesh
At the cutout of his knee brace
Was like a dick in a fist.

I said no

I said yes
I said no
Wasn't happy.

I never get these.

And the Christ said
Eloi, Eloi, lama sabachthani.

Anyway
It doesn't matter
What happens in
My life it's
My life.

I'll never hate it.

Still,
I don't want it revealed I'm uptight.
(I'm uptight.)
Sigh.
There was a point when if I had to get
One of the hot deli pastas I'd get the large one.
These days I get the small. (And a Limonata.)
I can eat my pasta on a blanket in the park
Alone.
People will or won't
Stare at me.
I'm practising.

I have to live
In the day
At the park
Being
Looked at
Even.

So I have a brand new set of markers

And a couple bags of chips.

Yea, my hand is not steady

But my heart wet

And lithe.

Lend me your neck or your palm

And I will draw something ugly by accident.

Five

I was a born a baby.

I didn't have any teeth.
My favourite lady
Was there.
I cried
Due to the fact of
Air.

Her hair was thick and waved
And black and mellow.
My boots have holes.
She buys me high-tops.

The allegory of the $50 high-tops.

At first they felt too full the ankle support
Overwhelming
And now I am like
Heel cushioning: Praise God.
Let's hope no one destroys me.

Also I need a costume.
I made a dance; I need a costume.
What can I wear?
That will show my clavicle
But cover my tiddies.

Eighteen degrees Celsius
Zagora
No events
Mostly cloudy

It was as fake as most movies. I loved the final shot.
It was a puritanical film.
The conceit of the vampire author genius
Musician genius
Was heavy-handed
And stupid. Also,
Tangiers
Is not like that.

It's January.
The water
In the pool
At the back
Of the auberge
Is cold.
Still,
I sit beside it.

I sit in a tent.
It is a square tent.
I am joined by a hungry peacock.
And then
I am joined by a
Large bandaged dog.

In a green pleated skirt I pass a forest of palms
The roads eyelashed in sand.
Children look
From my face
To my high-tops
To my face. I like it.
I get
What I come for.

Do I tell you?

The goat

He has to bray.
To pull his rope leash in the light.
He did it again in the black-blue sky
Of my leaving.
It is death.
He has to fucking bray
Because he is alive
And
Tied up.

I asked Fadwa what
A phrase meant;
It had hooked my bad ear and what
She said is it meant
You should be
Shy.

And then Manuela said my buns were horns
Were my tied-up
Sex.
I released them.
Je ne sais pas how to say this en anglais mais
My selves:
I suppose we
Gave me a course
Making our soul of a fitness enough
To scorn you
But not enough to
Not scorn you –
D'accord?

I cut my horns

And bray.
I'm not evil.
It's true:
I saw a demon.
It was a donkey.
Loose
At the desert
Before dawn.
If I'm to be honest, I'm
Not even sure it was a donkey.
It was a demon.
I'm sorry but also
I'm not
Even fucking kidding.

My anger is hope for my own righteousness.

I have to be angry to have any hope of being good.
For anything to mean I have to
Be angry, i.e., sad
I have to
Weep so I don't
Die.

The coo of the common emerald dove is the sound of Venus.

I love everyone I ever have and always will.

A performance called DON'T YOU WANNA KNOW WHAT I'M DOING EVERY DAY!

I have to live lest I die-live.

R. says he wants to be here til 250, but
He's young.
M. says by then he plans on
Being
Somewhere else.
I have to
Live here while I
Can.

When I die
I'll just be
Me again –
And soft.

I was will
Have been
Born
A baby.

It's why I was born.

I was named that.
I make it so that I like to.
I'm sort of damn good at it.
Anyway, I'm here.

Might as well.

Six

I told you.

The water is my special place.

I've been to the ocean and
I've been to the sea.

At the shore, the water greets me with its
Constancy.

I look it in the wave.
And know forever love.

How much of your body is your head.

Think about it.
How much of your body is your legs.
These are some of the ways I've been
Instructed.
Proportions
Are information, okay?

For instance
I have very long fingers.

The trick to being funny by Aisha Sasha John.

The trick to being funny is never joking.

I couldn't win with my brother because I was born.

And I couldn't win with my dad
Because my
Mother made me.

She named me living.

Thanks.

I cannot be ruined.

I've seen stuff always.

Everyone knows what
Everything means
All the time.

I have to be angry
So as not to be
Confused.

I have to sing.

So I don't die.

For you and all your siblings and friends and husbands or boyfriends.

I pray God increase your speed, decrease your speed, stop you all, and turn you all around in whatever direction you need to turn to avoid and to prevent you all from causing injuries, accidents, death, encounters with wild and/or dangerous domestic animals, and any other evil encounters, which only come to kill, to destroy, and to steal, from happening to others and to you all. And cause others to prevent and to avoid those same things from happening to others, to you all, and to themselves in Jesus' name.

With the love of God,

Daddy

Page 2 of 2

Seven

I removed the snake ring.

I put it back on.
Our body is God.

Pussy pain.

Bike crash.
Mid-thirties
Adolescent.

Monday morning.
I look at the shore.

I'm sheepish and lost.
I am so tired at the shore.
Jesus is waiting.

The reassuring thing about life

Is that no matter how things turn out
I still get to be Aisha Sasha John.

At the very least I have that
Honour always.

Although last week I was pissed.

Psychic = Self-believer

I left the liquor store at Bloor and Ossington grumpy.
I said Lord give me beauty | I bumped into Marvin.
It's most comfortable to be in
Direct relation to the song's rhythm and mood.

In which the other dancers rise when I drop and vice versa.
Dance as continuously getting more comfortable
In the form of
Listening to music together.

The year of being selfish. The year of being relaxed.

I am eating someone else's cashews.

I think it was smart of whoever's idea I am
To be me.

I find the book.

I read it.

What do
Uh I wear to the show?

I get my power from pleasure.
And I get my pleasure from pleasure, too.

I get my power from knowing
The way to have the most pleasure

Is to have the most pleasure.

I'm on the back of something.

And it's carrying me.
I have to live as a traveller.
I close my eyes.

And I see.

I'm not dead.

A person named "Jonathan Valelly" asked me to
Do something I did not want to
Do and so I did not do
It
Because I don't care (it is cold outside)
(I have snot in my nose) plus I
Don't give a
Fuck.

An oval on my pant leg of oil.

The world its lips
Get on me.

The sweet and cold
Wet of the world.

Lay it down
By Al Green featuring someone else.

I don't want no-
Body else,

He sings
Lay it down.

Let it go.
Fall in love, he says/sings.

Of things evil as well as good
Long intercourse

Induces love.

I'm not gonna die of love.

And I'm not
Gonna die for shame.

Except I will die of love thank God.

My heaven meets me in the day.

My heaven meets me in

Your company

And yours.

And yours.

And yours.

And also

Yours, hi.

I have to live.
I'm married to love.

The spirit
Is the body.

Acknowledgements

Thank you for your love and conversation:
Mom, Marvin, Alexis, Nadia, Steve, Julia, Mayko
Dionne, Jim, Andrea, Emerson, Anita, Andrea

and to the spirits Esme Bailey and Colin Anthony.